+
597.96
H835bL
2012

FOND DU LAC PUBLIC LIBRARY

WITHDRAWN

MAR 06 2012

WILD ABOUT SNAKES

BLACK MAMBAS

BY MELANIE A. HOWARD

Consultants:
Joe Maierhauser, President/CEO
Terry Phillip, Curator of Reptiles
Reptile Gardens
Rapid City, South Dakota

CAPSTONE PRESS
a capstone imprint

Edge Books are published by Capstone Press,
151 Good Counsel Drive, P.O. Box 669, Mankato, Minnesota 56002.
www.capstonepub.com

Copyright © 2012 by Capstone Press, a Capstone imprint.
All rights reserved.
No part of this publication may be reproduced in whole or in part,
or stored in a retrieval system, or transmitted in any form or by any means,
electronic, mechanical, photocopying, recording, or otherwise, without
written permission of the publisher.
For information regarding permission, write to Capstone Press,
151 Good Counsel Drive, P.O. Box 669, Dept. R, Mankato, Minnesota 56002.

Books published by Capstone Press are manufactured with paper containing at least 10 percent post-consumer waste.

Library of Congress Cataloging-in-Publication Data
Howard, Melanie A.
  Black mambas / by Melanie A. Howard.
    p. cm. — (Wild about snakes)
  Includes index.
  ISBN 978-1-4296-6012-9 (library binding)
  ISBN 978-1-4296-7281-8 (paperback)
  1. Black mamba—Juvenile literature. I. Title.
  QL666.O64H67 2012
  597.96'2—dc22   2011010344

Editorial Credits
Brenda Haugen, editor; Ted Williams, designer; Eric Manske, production specialist

Photo Credits
Alamy: Andrew Hewitt, 15, Naturepix, 16; Ardea.com: Adrian Warren, 22; CORBIS: epa/Vassil Donev, 21, Gallo Images/Anthony Bannister, 23, Gallo Images/Rob C. Nunnington, 18; Dreamstime: Fotandy, 28-29, Robin Winkelman, 1; Getty Images Inc.: Gallo Images/Rod Patterson, cover, National Geographic/Beverly Joubert, 5; iStockphoto: Gary Martin, 12-13, Mark Kostich, 8; Photolibrary: Peter Arnold Images/R. Andrew Odum, 25; Photoshot Holdings: NHPA/Anthony Bannister, 6; Super Stock Inc.: Animals Animals, 10-11, 26

Artistic Effects
Shutterstock: Marilyn Volan

TABLE OF CONTENTS

LEGENDARY MONSTERS	4
MAMBAS INSIDE OUT	8
ON THE PROWL	16
BLACK MAMBAS AND PEOPLE	24

Glossary 30
Read More 31
Internet Sites 31
Index 32

Chapter 1
LEGENDARY MONSTERS

Twenty workers stand in the dirt outside a sugarcane field in Swaziland, a small country in southern Africa. They will not go back to working in the field. One of them spotted a snake slithering through the spiky leaves. He thinks it's a black mamba.

The workers' fear is common. Legends about black mambas are spread all across Africa. Some people believe black mambas have magical abilities. Others say a black mamba can roll downhill like a wheel by biting its own tail. Then the snake attacks with super speed. Some people believe a black mamba can balance on the tip of its tail. There are even myths about black mambas creating terrible whirlwinds with their speed and power.

Some people think black mambas are crafty and plan attacks on humans. Some believe a black mamba will wait at the side of the road for a car to come by. Then the snake will wrap itself around one of the car's wheels and bite the driver when the car stops.

Humans are not alone in fearing black mambas. A black mamba can make a herd of African buffalo and even rhinoceroses scatter by displaying its attack warning signs. Black mambas most likely act defensively toward these animals to avoid being trampled.

Beware of the Bite

With so many scary stories being told, it's no wonder the black mamba is one of the most feared snakes in the world. And black mambas have not been studied as much as other snakes. This makes them seem even more mysterious. But the stories are just that—stories.

Black mambas are fierce when they are cornered. But they do not hunt humans, and they do not have magical abilities. A black mamba can move with a third of its body off the ground, but it cannot balance on the tip of its tail. And it certainly will not roll downhill.

Black mambas on or near the road are in danger of being run over. They can't ride on car wheels. And though they are fast, they don't make whirlwinds.

A black mamba bite is known as the Kiss of Death.

What really makes a black mamba so scary is its bite. Black mambas are among the world's most dangerous snakes because they release deadly **venom** through their bites. Just two drops of black mamba venom can kill a human.

venom—a toxic substance produced by some snakes

Africa's Deadliest Snakes

Africa is home to many dangerous snakes besides black mambas. Some of the most dangerous are the boomslang, the puff adder, and the saw-scaled viper.

The boomslang is the most venomous rear-fanged snake in the world. It can open its mouth as wide as 170 degrees to bite.

Puff adders puff up when they get anxious. Their venomous bites can kill people.

Many agree that the most dangerous snake in Africa is the saw-scaled viper. It has a more toxic venom than the black mamba, and it causes many more deaths. Saw-scaled vipers are easily stepped on, since they blend in with their surroundings. They often live close to human populations and are quick to bite.

Chapter 2

MAMBAS INSIDE OUT

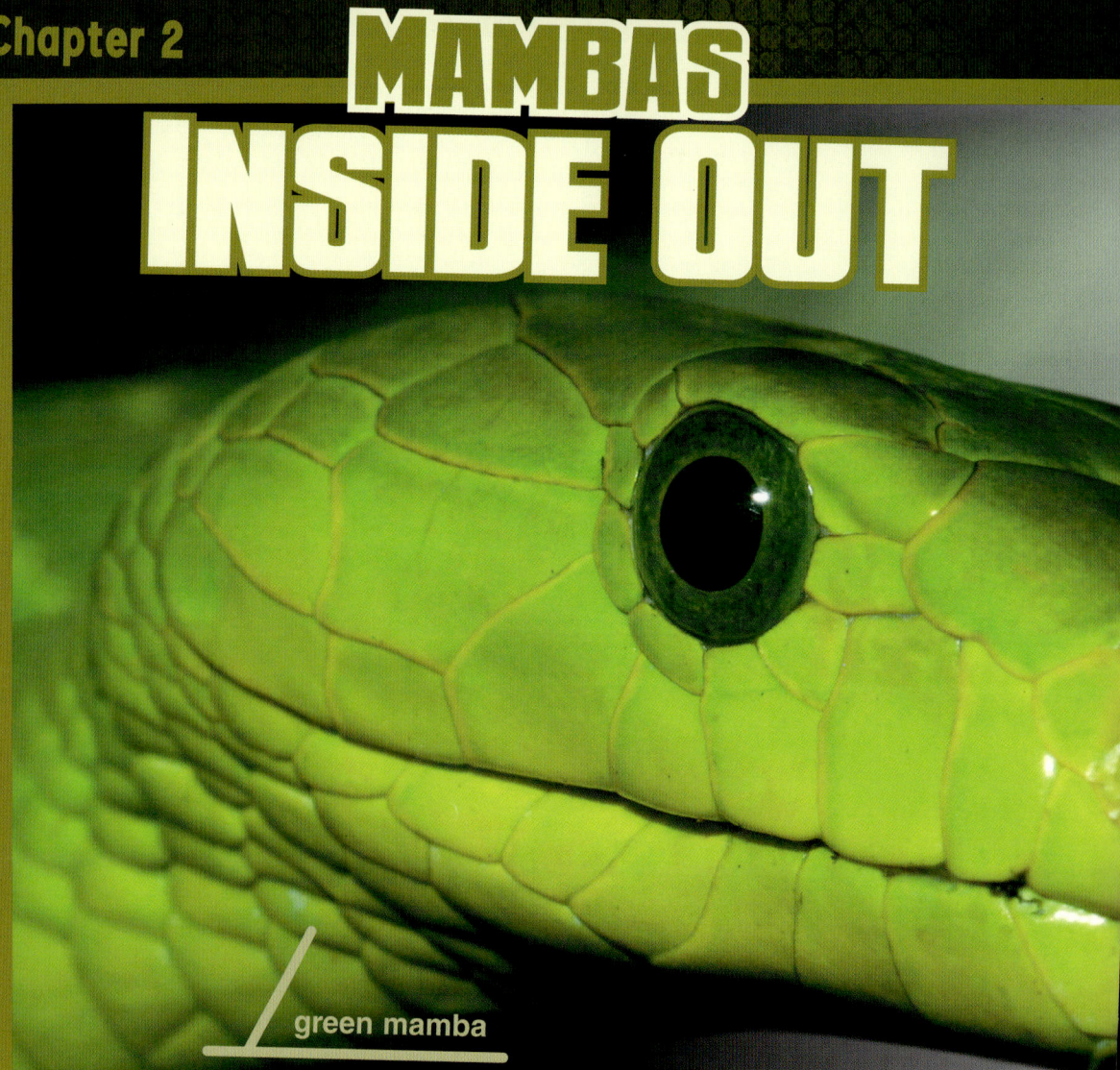

green mamba

Like all other snakes, black mambas are **reptiles**. Black mambas belong to a group of snakes called mambas. The mambas include four **species** of snakes. They are the East African green mamba, the West African green mamba, the black mamba, and Jameson's mamba.

Mambas belong to a larger family of snakes called *Elapidae*. This family contains other deadly snakes, such as cobras. Unlike vipers, which can fold their fangs down from the roof of their mouths for use, elapid fangs are fixed in position.

Black mambas live only in Africa. Their range extends from South Africa all the way up the east coast to Somalia and Ethiopia. Black mambas can be found as far west as Senegal.

Black Mamba Range
□ where black mambas live

reptile—a cold-blooded animal that breathes air and has a backbone; most reptiles lay eggs and have scaly skin
species—a specific type of animal or plant

The black mamba is a good swimmer. But it doesn't like to spend time in water.

Home Sweet Home

Black mambas live in grasslands and rocky, hilly areas. They like to make their homes in deserted holes in the ground, hollow tree trunks, or termite mounds. As long as the area is not disturbed, a black mamba will return to its home regularly.

A black mamba is as comfortable in a tree as it is on the ground. Its light-colored belly helps it blend in against the sky. The snake's **prey** could look up and not see a black mamba resting in a treetop. If the trees in a wooded area are close enough together, a black mamba can travel without returning to the ground. It can stretch its long body over distances of 3 feet (91 centimeters) or more.

prey—an animal hunted by another for food

Giants on the Go

Black mambas can reach lengths of about 14 feet (4.3 meters). But most are about 8 feet (2.4 m) long. The black mamba is Africa's largest venomous snake. It is the second longest venomous snake in the world. The king cobra is the longest. The black mamba usually raises its body off the ground in order to strike.

Being big does not make this snake slow. It can travel at speeds up to 12.5 miles (20 kilometers) per hour. It is among the fastest snakes in the world.

The average height of an American male is 5 feet 10 inches (178 centimeters)

Green Mambas

Of the four snakes that belong to the mambas, three of them are green. Like the black mamba, the East African green mamba, the West African green mamba, and Jameson's mamba are active during the day. They have coffin-shaped heads and are venomous. Unlike black mambas, green mambas spend little time on the ground. They prefer to live and hunt in trees.

Green mambas don't grow as long as black mambas. An adult green mamba is usually about 5 to 9 feet (1.5 to 2.7 meters) long.

Humans do not see green mambas as often as black mambas. Green mambas are more shy than black mambas. It's rare for a person who is not a snake handler to be bitten by a green mamba.

Skin Deep

A black mamba's skin is not black. Its scales may range in color from light gray to dark olive green to gray-brown. The snakes are called black mambas because the insides of their mouths are very dark, almost black.

Like all snakes, the black mamba sheds its skin regularly. Snakes shed for a few reasons. The most common reason is that they have outgrown their old skin. A snake's skin does not grow as the snake grows. Snakes start the shedding process by rubbing their noses against rough surfaces. Then they slowly wriggle out of the old skin by moving against tree bark, rocks, or brush. Another reason snakes shed is to heal after injuries. A snake that has been injured might shed several times to replace the damaged skin.

Female black mambas shed their skin before laying eggs.

Chapter 3
ON THE PROWL

Black mambas are active during the day. They spend much of their time sunning themselves. Snakes are cold-blooded. Their body temperatures change with their surroundings. Sunning helps a black mamba keep its body temperature at 86 degrees Fahrenheit (30 degrees Celsius). This is the perfect body temperature for a snake on the hunt. If its body temperature is too low, the snake cannot move as quickly. If the snake gets too warm, it could suffer heat exhaustion. Staying the ideal temperature keeps a snake's nerves, muscles, and digestive system working at the best possible level.

A black mamba will often sun itself before it goes hunting. It might lie on a tree branch in the sun for hours. A black mamba often returns to the same spot to sun itself every day.

Sensing Prey

Black mambas "smell" prey with their tongues. The snake's tongue darts out and collects scent particles. When it pulls its tongue back in, the snake puts the fork of its tongue into holes at the top of its mouth. The holes are openings to the **Jacobson's organ**. The Jacobson's organ helps the snake's brain decode the scents. The snakes can then detect a possible meal.

Jacobson's organ—an organ on the roof of the mouth of a reptile that helps identify scents

Basketball player Kobe Bryant is known as the "Black Mamba." He says this is because "The mamba can strike with 99 percent accuracy at maximum speed, in rapid succession. That's the kind of basketball precision I want to have."

What's for Dinner?

Black mambas are patient hunters. They prefer to track and attack their prey. Other types of snakes will wait for prey to come to them. Black mambas go out in search of prey.

Black mambas have excellent eyesight. They can clearly see prey while striking.

Black mambas eat squirrels and other rodents. They will also eat young birds and lizards. A black mamba will strike its prey at least once to get venom into it. What the snake does next depends on what it's hunting. Usually a black mamba will strike its prey and then back off. It waits for the animal to die from the venom before it eats the prey. But if the black mamba is hunting a bird, the snake will hold on to the bird so it can't fly away.

Venom

A black mamba's venom **paralyzes** its prey. Muscles around its venom gland contract and squirt venom through the snake's hollow fangs. Paralyzing its prey helps keep the snake from getting scratched or bitten. In time the venom kills the prey.

Down the Hatch

A black mamba eats its prey whole. The snake usually tries to swallow its prey headfirst. That way the limbs of the prey fold in naturally, making it easier to eat.

A black mamba can eat prey bigger than its head. Flexible tissue connects the two halves of the snake's lower jaw. The tissue allows a snake's mouth to open wide.

paralyze—to cause a loss of the ability to control the muscles

Prowling for a Mate

The black mambas' mating season begins in the spring. During mating season two male black mambas will often fight over a female. The goal is not to kill each other. The two snakes twist around each other and wrestle. When one pins the other to the ground, the fight is over. The winner earns the right to mate with the female.

Black mambas are **oviparous**, which means they lay eggs. Female black mambas lay between six and 17 eggs in the summer. They prefer to lay their eggs in a nest underground or in a hollow tree. The eggs hatch in about three months.

Black mambas are between 16 and 24 inches (40 and 60 cm) when they hatch. They grow quickly. A young snake may grow up to 6 feet (2 m) in its first year. After it hatches, a black mamba is ready to take care of itself.

Young and Shy

Young black mambas are easily spooked. They are rarely seen by people. Their shy nature helps them survive because it helps them escape **predators**. Many young black mambas are eaten by birds or other snakes.

oviparous—describes an animal that lays eggs that develop and hatch outside the female's body

predator—an animal that hunts other animals for food

Black Mambas and People

Black mambas are among the snakes most feared by people. Black mambas have some of the deadliest snake venom. Yet they are responsible for few human deaths. It is difficult to say exactly how many people are killed by black mamba bites each year. Black mambas live in areas where there are many kinds of venomous snakes. They also live close to villages that are far from medical care.

Warning Signals

A black mamba won't attack a person without warning. Black mambas are shy by nature. If threatened, a black mamba will try to escape. But if it is cornered, a black mamba is not afraid to fight. It will rear up off the ground. Then it will flatten its neck into a hood and open its mouth wide. It often waves its tongue slowly up and down and hisses.

If a person or predator moves suddenly when a black mamba gives these signals, the snake will probably bite. A black mamba will often strike more than once. It can strike as high as an adult's face.

As many as 20,000 people are killed by snakebites every year.

Bites to People

The toxins in a black mamba's venom affect its victim's heart and lungs. The venom can kill a person in six to 15 hours. If the snake injects a lot of venom in its bite, a person could die in as little as 20 minutes. Someone who has been bitten should be taken to a hospital right away. Doctors can treat snakebite victims with **antivenom**.

antivenom—a medicine that helps the body fight off the effects of animal venom

Human Threat to Mambas

There are few predators that are a threat to the black mamba. An adult black mamba has little to fear from anything but humans. In Africa people are moving into areas where black mambas live. Black mambas have been found in schools, hotels, fields, and homes. Many people are afraid of black mambas and believe the myths about them. When they find black mambas, people often try to kill them rather than find a way to get them back into the wild safely.

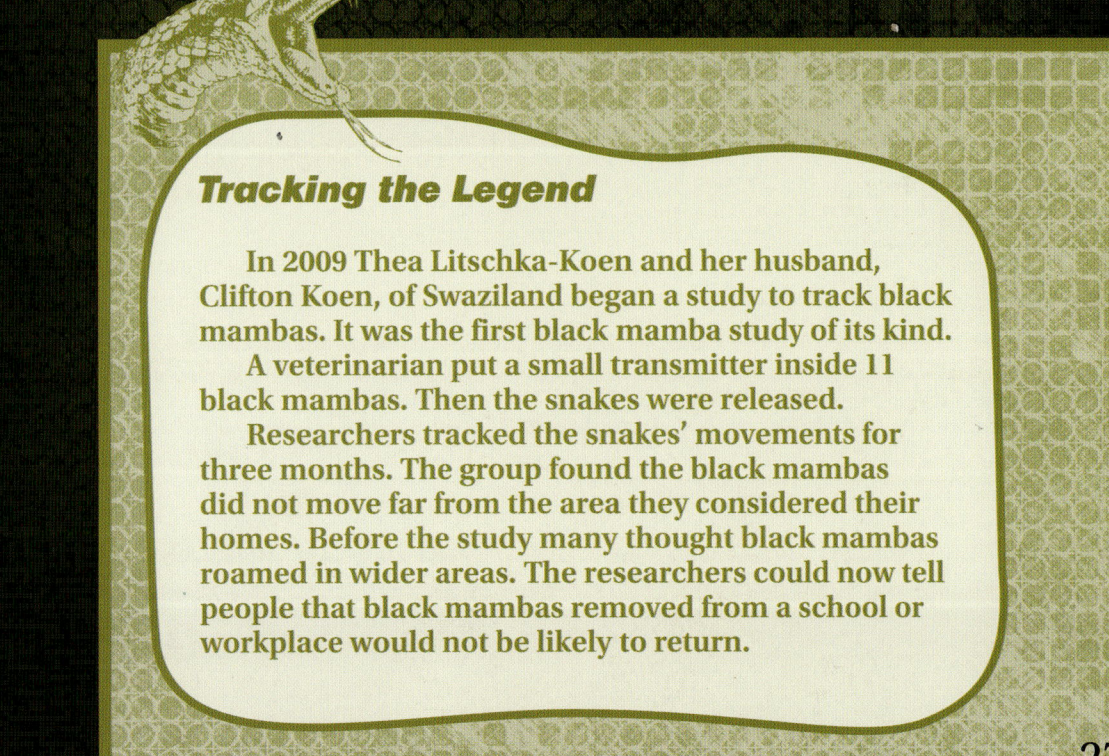

Tracking the Legend

In 2009 Thea Litschka-Koen and her husband, Clifton Koen, of Swaziland began a study to track black mambas. It was the first black mamba study of its kind.

A veterinarian put a small transmitter inside 11 black mambas. Then the snakes were released.

Researchers tracked the snakes' movements for three months. The group found the black mambas did not move far from the area they considered their homes. Before the study many thought black mambas roamed in wider areas. The researchers could now tell people that black mambas removed from a school or workplace would not be likely to return.

Respecting the Mamba

Black mambas are fast, fierce creatures. They might seem scary, but they serve an important purpose. Like most snakes, they keep other animal populations from becoming too large. They help keep the rodent population down by hunting and eating animals such as rats and squirrels. Rodents can carry diseases that make people sick.

Efforts have begun to educate people about snakes such as the black mamba. Scientists have also started to study the mysterious snake more closely. As people understand more about these snakes, they will gain more respect for the amazing animals they are.

GLOSSARY

antivenom (an-tee-VEN-uhm)—a medicine that helps the body fight off the effects of animal venom

Jacobson's organ (JAY-kub-suhns OR-guhn)—an organ on the roof of the mouth of a reptile that helps identify scents

oviparous (OH-vip-a-rus)—describes an animal that lays eggs that develop and hatch outside the female's body

paralyze (PAY-ruh-lize)—to cause a loss of the ability to control the muscles

predator (PRED-uh-tur)—an animal that hunts other animals for food

prey (PRAY)—an animal hunted by another for food

reptile (REP-tile)—a cold-blooded animal that breathes air and has a backbone; most reptiles lay eggs and have scaly skin

species (SPEE-sheez)—a specific type of animal or plant

venom (VEN-uhm)—a toxic substance produced by some snakes

READ MORE

Gangemi, Angelo. *Black Mamba.* Killer Snakes. New York: Gareth Stevens Publishing, 2011.

Menon, Sujatha. *Discover Snakes.* Berkeley Heights, N.J.: Enslow Publishing, 2009.

White, Nancy. *Black Mambas: Sudden Death!* Fangs. New York: Bearport Publishing, 2009.

INTERNET SITES

FactHound offers a safe, fun way to find Internet sites related to this book. All of the sites on FactHound have been researched by our staff.

Here's all you do:

Visit *www.facthound.com*

Type in this code: 9781429660129

Check out projects, games and lots more at
www.capstonekids.com

INDEX

antivenom, 26

biting. *See* striking.
body temperatures, 16–17
boomslangs, 7
Bryant, Kobe, 19

cobras, 9, 12
colors, 11, 13, 14

diseases, 28

East African green mambas, 8, 13
eggs, 14, 23
Elapidae family, 9
eyesight, 19

fangs, 7, 9, 20
fighting, 22

hatching, 23
homes, 10, 11, 13, 27
hunting, 6, 11, 13, 16, 17, 19, 28

injuries, 14

Jacobson's organ, 18
Jameson's mambas, 8, 13
jaws, 20

Koen, Clifton, 27

Litschka-Koen, Thea, 27

mating, 22
myths, 4, 6, 27

predators, 23, 25, 27
prey, 11, 18, 19, 20, 28
puff adders, 7

saw-scaled vipers, 7
scales, 14
senses, 18, 19
shedding, 14
shyness, 13, 23, 24
sizes, 12, 13, 23
skin, 14
speed, 4, 12, 19
stretching, 11
striking, 4, 7, 12, 13, 19, 20, 24, 25, 26
sunning, 16–17
swallowing, 20

teeth. *See* fangs.
tongue, 18, 24
trees, 10, 11, 13, 14, 17, 23

venom, 7, 12, 13, 19, 20, 24, 26

West African green mambas, 8, 13